In the Pit

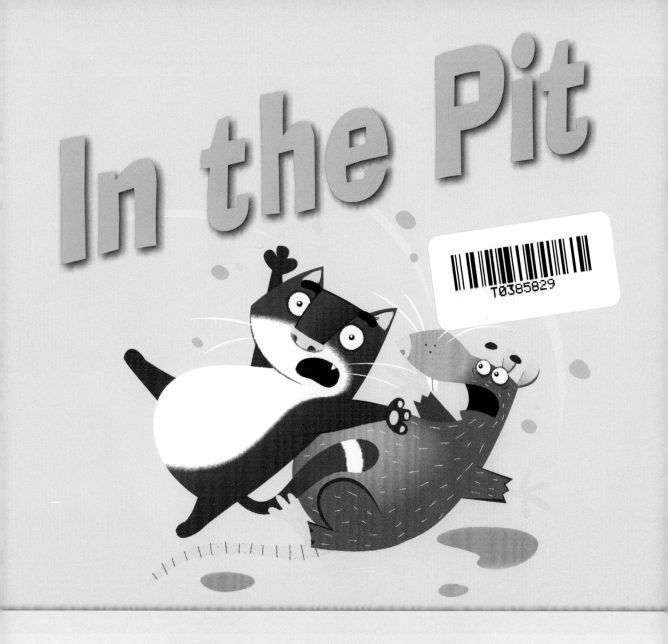

Written by Monica Hughes

Illustrated by Gabriele Antonini

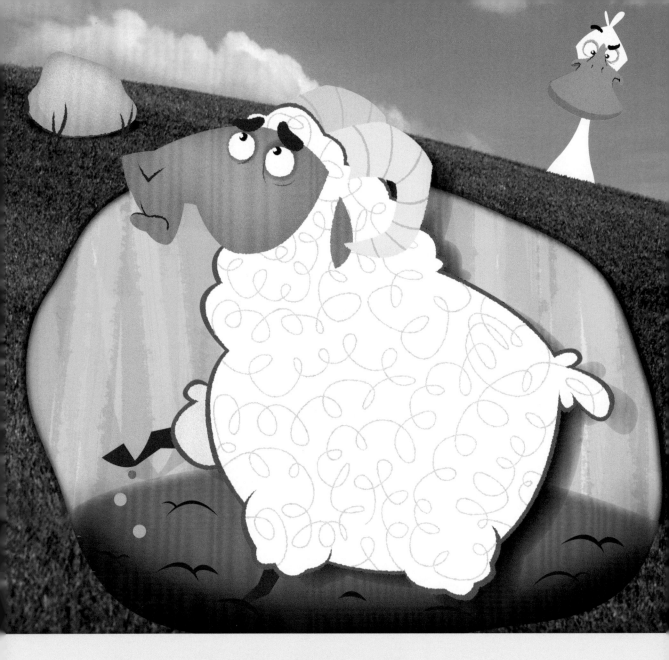

Ram is in the pit.

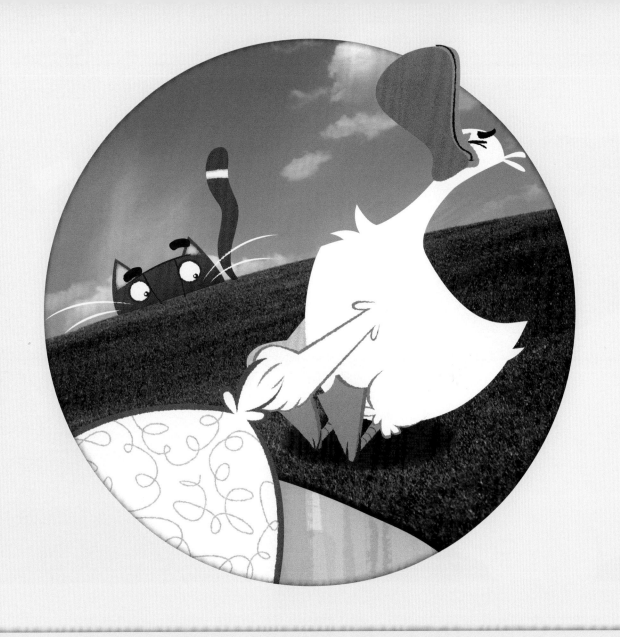

Duck tugs at Ram.

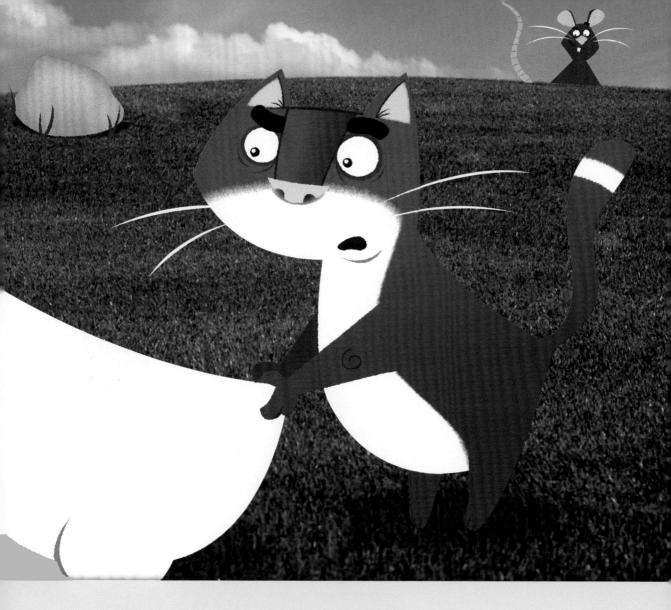

Cat tugs at Duck.

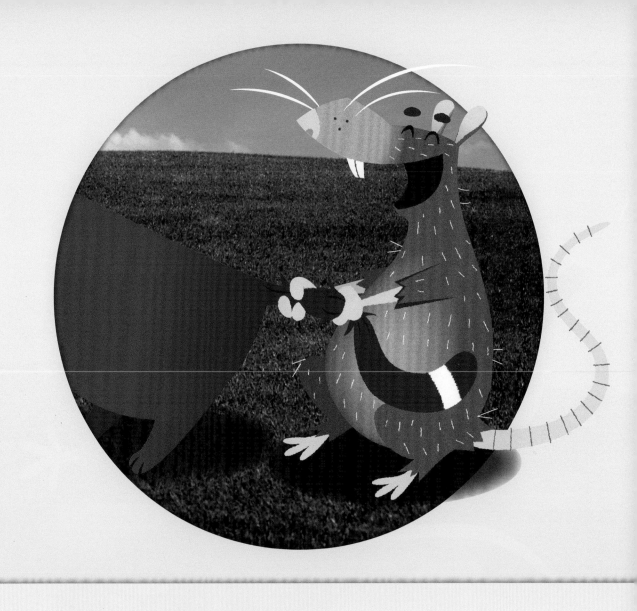

Rat tugs at Cat.
"Go on, Rat!"

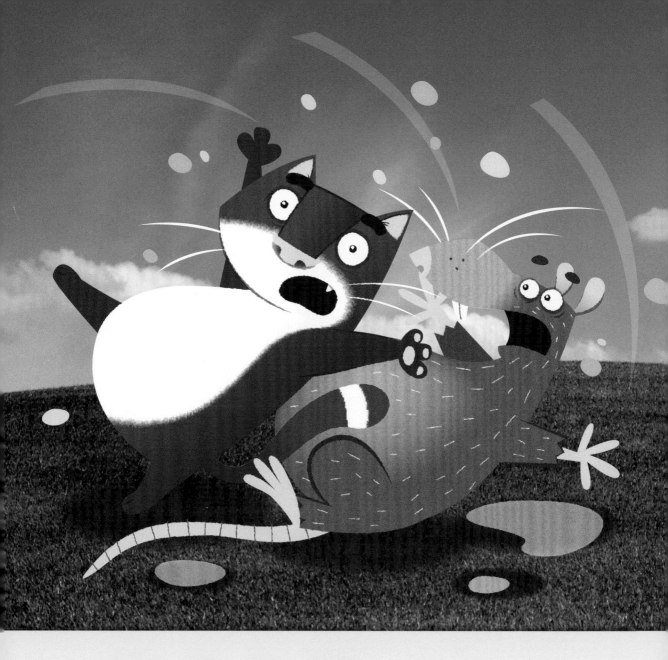

Cat sits on Rat.

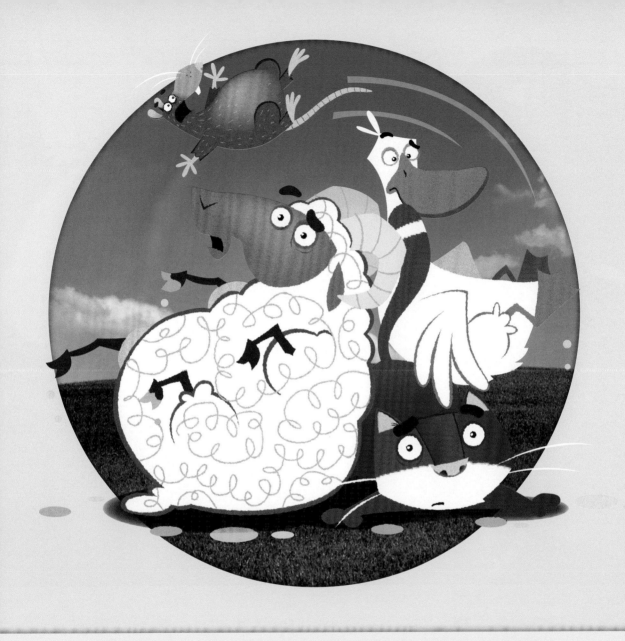

Ram and Duck sit on Cat.

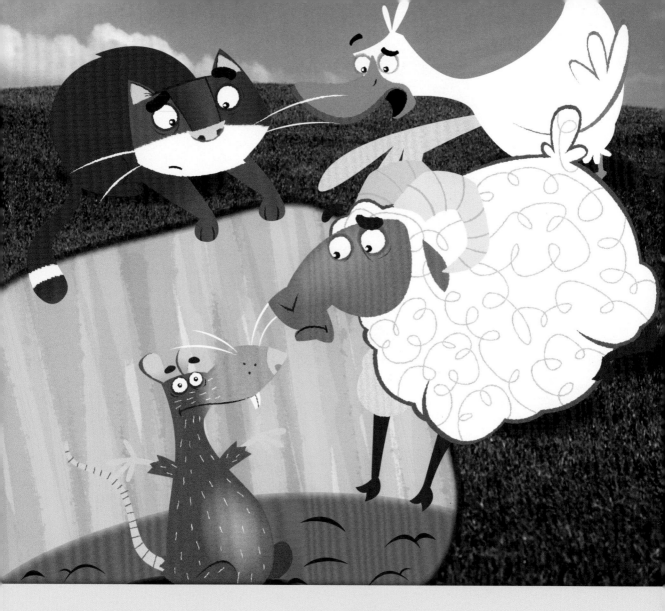

Can Ram get Rat?
No! Rat is in the pit.